Contents

Chapter 1: Naming and using variables:

Avoid using python keywords and function names as variable names

Chapter 2: Strings

1-Changing case in a string with methods:

```
name = "erwin smith"
print(name.title())
        output
Erwin Smith
```

A method is an action that python performs on a piece of data. The dot(.) after name in name.title tells python to make the title() method act on the variable name.

We could've used also:

```
print(name.upper())
print(name.lower()) #useful for storing data
```

2-Combining and concatenating strings:

```
first_name = "erwin"
last_name = "smith"
full_name = first_name + " " + last_name
message = "the commander of the scouts " \
        + full_name.title() + " was a great leader!"
print(message)

        output:
the commander of the scouts Erwin Smith was a great lead
er!
```

3-Adding white space to strings with tabs or newlines:

```
print("erwin")
print("\terwin")
        output
erwin
    erwin
```

4-Adding a new line:

```
print("Characters:\nerwin \nlevi \nhange")
        output
Characters:
erwin
levi
hange
```

5-Stripping whitespace (recovering white space):

```
favorit_character = "    erwin    "
print(favorit_character.rstrip())
        output
    erwin#removed the spaces from the right side only

favorit_character = "    erwin    "
print(favorit_character.lstrip())
        output
erwin    #removed the spaces from the left side only

favorit_character = "    erwin    "
print(favorit_character.strip())
        output
erwin #removed spaces from both sides
```

Chapter 3: Lists

In python square brackets [] indicates a list, and individual elements in the list are separated by comas ( ) so it should be like this:

```
List = ["...", "...", "..."]
```

1-Accessing Elements in a list:

```
characters = ["reiner", "bertholt", "annie", "zeke"]
print(characters[0])
      output
reiner

print(characters[0].title())
      output
Reiner
```

Note:

1. Index position starts at 0 not 1
2. Python has a special syntax for accessing the last element in a list. By asking for the item at index -1.

```
print(characters[-1])
      output
zeke

print(characters[-2])
      output
annie
```

2-Using individual values from a list:

```
characters = ["reiner", "bertholt", "annie", "zeke"]
message = "fun fact I discovered who is " \
        + characters[0].title() \
        + " before watching season 2"
print(message)
        output
fun fact I discovered who is Reiner before watching seas
on 2
```

3-Modifying elements in a list:

```
characters = ["reiner", "bertholt", "annie", "zeke"]
characters[0]="ymir"
print(characters)
        output
['ymir', 'bertholt', 'annie', 'zeke']
```

4-Adding elements in a list:

```
characters.append("eren")
        output
['ymir', 'bertholt', 'annie', 'zeke', 'eren']
```

5-Inserting elements to a list:

```
characters.insert(0, "eren")
        output
['eren', 'ymir', 'bertholt', 'annie', 'zeke']
```

6-Removing elements from a list using the function del:

```
del characters[0]
        output
['bertholt', 'annie', 'zeke']
```

9

7-Removing an item using the pop method:

The pop() method removes the last item but it lets you work with it after removing it. *(you can still put the index of the item needed inside the parenthesis if you want to pop a specific item)*

```
print(characters)
popped_character = characters.pop()
print(characters)
print(popped_character)
      output
['ymir', 'bertholt', 'annie', 'zeke']
['ymir', 'bertholt', 'annie']
zeke #you can still use zeke even though he is popped
off the list
```

useful use:

```
characters = ["reiner", "bertholt", "annie", "zeke"]
last_character = characters.pop()
print("the last character shown in season two is "\
     + last_character.title())
      Output
the last character shown in season two is Zeke
```

note:

use pop() if you want to use an item as you remove it.
use del() if you don't want the item any more.

8-Removing an item by value:

```
characters = ["reiner", "bertholt", "annie", "zeke"]
characters.remove("bertholt")
print(characters)
        output
['reiner', 'annie', 'zeke']
```

note:

you can also use the remove() method to work with a value that's being removed from a list.

```
characters = ["reiner", "bertholt", "annie", "zeke"]
the_beast = "zeke"
characters.remove(the_beast)
print("the beast titan is " + the_beast.title())
        output
the beast titan is Zeke
```

9-Organizing a list:
Sorting a list with the sort method (permanently):

1. Alphabetical order: List.sort()
2. Reverse alphabetical order:
   List.sort(reverse=True)

Sorting a list temporarily using the function sorted():

1. Alphabetical order: sorted(list)
2. Reverse alphabetical order:
   sorted(list, reverse=True)

note:

Sorting a list is a bit more complicated when all values are not in lowercase

10-Printing a list in reverse order (permanently):

To reverse a list we use the `reverse()` method.

note:

> 1. The reverse method does note take care of alphabetical order, it just reverses the list
> 2. If we want the list to its original order after using the `reverse()` method we just need to use the method one more time

11-Finding the length of a list:

```
characters = ["reiner", "bertholt", "annie", "zeke"]
print(len(characters))
        output
4
```

note:

> the `len()` method counts the items starting by 1

12-important ideas for using len() method:

you'll find the `len()` method useful when you need to figure out the number of registered users in a website, determine the amount of data you have to manage in visualization…etc

13-Avoiding index error when working with lists:

```
IndexError: list index out of range
```

1. When this error occurs, it means that python can't figure out the item you requested, so try adjusting the index number by 1.
2. You can have this error appear when you ask for the last item in `print(characters[-1])` but only if your list is empty

Chapter 4: Working with lists

1-Looping through an entire list:

```python
characters = ["reiner", "bertholt", "annie", "zeke"]
for character in characters:
    print(character.title())
        output
Reiner
Bertholt
Annie
Zeke
```

2-important ideas for using the for loop:

when you're processing data using the `for` loop, you'll find that this is a great way to summarize an operation that was performed on an entire data. For example, in a game...you can use it to show all characters of a game after that show the play button.

3-Making numerical lists:
important ideas for making numerical lists:

- Keep track of each character's position in a game
- Keep track of each player's high score
- In data visualization as temperature, distances population sizes, latitude, longitude...and more

4-Using the range() function:

```
for cadets in range(1,4):
    print(cadets)
        output
1
2
3
```

5-Using range() to make a list of numbers:

We need to convert the range() function using the list() function:

```
cadets = list(range(1, 4))
print(cadets)
        output
[1, 2, 3]
```

We can use the range() function to tell python to skip numbers in a giver range. For example this is how we would list the even numbers between 1 and 10.

```
even_numbers = list(range(2,11,2))
print(even_numbers)
        output
[2, 4, 6, 8, 10]
```

6-Simple statics with a list of numbers:

Finding the minimum, maximum and sum of a list using functions.

```
min(list)
max(list)
sum(list)
```

7-list comprehensions:

crating a list that shows the square numbers from 1-10.

Ordinary way:

```
square = []
for scout in range(1,11):#scout is just an AoT reference
    square.append(scout**2)
print(square)
      output
[1, 4, 9, 16, 25, 36, 49, 64, 81, 100]
```

Using list comprehensions:

```
square = [scout**2 for scout in range (1,11)]
print(square)
      output
[1, 4, 9, 16, 25, 36, 49, 64, 81, 100]
```

To use this syntax:

1. Descriptive name for the list
2. Open square brackets
3. Define the expression for the value you want to store in the list. Like in this example scout**2.
4. Write the for loop to generate the numbers you want to feed into the expression. The for loop in this example is for scout in range (1,11)] which feeds the value 1 through 10 into the expression

15

`scout**2`, notice that no column is used at the
end of the for statement.

8-Working with part of a list:
Working with a specific group of items in a list called
a slice.

9-Slicing a list:
As in `range()` the of by one rule applies in slice.

```
scouts = ["eren", "armin", "mikasa", "jean", "marco"]
print(scouts[0:3])
print(scouts[1:4])
print(scouts[:4])
print(scouts[2:])
print(scouts[-3:])
        output
['eren', 'armin', 'mikasa']
['armin', 'mikasa', 'jean']
['eren', 'armin', 'mikasa', 'jean']
['mikasa', 'jean', 'marco']
['mikasa', 'jean', 'marco']
```

10-Important idea for slice[-3:]
this could be used to print the name of the last three
players in a roaster.

11-Copying a list:

```
scouts = ["eren", "armin", "mikasa", "jean", "marco"]
cadets_104 = scouts[:]
print(cadets_104)
        output
['eren', 'armin', 'mikasa', 'jean', 'marco']
```

12-Tuples:

Tuple are just the same as lists but they cannot be modified.

To write a tuple we use ( ) instead of [ ]

note:

although we can't modify a tuple, we can assign a new value to the variable that holds a tuple.

```
scouts = ("eren", "armin", "mikasa")
scouts = ("zeke", "armin", "mikasa")
print(scouts)
        output
('zeke', 'armin', 'mikasa')
```

Chapter 5: If statement:

note:

sometimes it is useful to not use the else statement at the end of an if statement, and just use an elif instead, and by that you'll make sure that your program will work with correct info only.

Testing a multiple conditions:

sometimes it's important to check all of the conditions of interests. To do this we need to use multiple statements if with np elif or else blocks.

```
scouts = ("armin", "mikasa")
if "eren" in scouts:
    print("Eren is here")
if "armin" in scouts:
    print("Armin is here")
if "mikasa" in scouts:
    print("Mikasa is here")

print("\nFinished checking for the protagonists")
        output
Armin is here
Mikasa is here

Finished checking for the protagonists
```

Chapter 6: Dictionaries:

1-A simple dictionary:

```
captain_levi = {"power" : "96", "agility" : "97"}
print(captain_levi["power"])
print(captain_levi["agility"])
        output
96
97
```

A **key-value** pair is a set of values associated with each other. When you provide a key, python returns the value associated with that key. Every key is connected to its value by a column, and individual **key-value** pairs are separated by commas. You can store as many key value pairs as you want in a dictionary.

The simples dictionary has exactly one **key-value** pair as below:

```
captain_levi = {"power" : "96"}
```

2-Adding new key-value pair to a dictionary:

```
captain_levi = {"power" : "96", "agility" : "97"}
captain_levi["intellect"] = 85
print(captain_levi)
     output
{'power': '96', 'agility': '97', 'intellect': 85}
```

3-Starting with an empty dictionary:

```
commander_erwin = {}
commander_erwin["power"] = 75
commander_erwin["agility"] = 70
commander_erwin["intellect"] = 97
print(commander_erwin)
     output
{'power': 75, 'agility': 70, 'intellect': 97}
```

note:

Typically, you'll use empty dictionaries when storing
user-supplied data in a dictionary or when you write
code that generates a large number of key-value pairs
automatically

4-Modifying values in a dictionary:

```
commander_erwin = {"power" : 75, "agility" : 70, "intell
ect" : 97}
commander_erwin["power"] = "unknown"
print(commander_erwin)
        output
{'power': 'unknown', 'agility': 70, 'intellect': 97}
```

5-Removing key-value pairs: (permanent)

```
commander_erwin = {"power" : 75,
                   "agility" : 70,
                   "intellect" : 97}

del commander_erwin["power"]
print(commander_erwin)
        output
{'agility': 70, 'intellect': 97}
```

6-Looping through all key-value pairs:

```
commander_erwin = {"agility" : 70,
                   "intellect" : 97}
for key, value in commander_erwin.items():
    print("\nKey: " + str(key))
    #str() converts the value inside it to a string
    print("value: " + str(value))
        output

Key: agility
value: 70

Key: intellect
value: 97
```

7-Looping through all the keys in a dictionary:

The `keys()` method is useful when you don't need to work with all of the values in a dictionary.

```python
mikasa = {"power" : 91,
          "agility" : 89,
          "intellect" : 80}
for ability in mikasa.keys():
    print(ability.title())
        output
Power
Agility
Intellect
```

Looping through a dictionary keys in order:

```python
for ability in sorted(mikasa.keys()):
    print(ability.title())
        output
Agility
Intellect
Power
```

8-Looping through all value in a dictionary:

```python
for ability in mikasa.values():
    print(ability)
        output
91
89
80
```

To ignore repetition, we use set() method:

```
mikasa = {"power" : 91,
          "agility" : 89,
          "intellect" : 80,
          "reflex" : 89}
for ability in set(mikasa.values()):
    print(ability)
        output
80
89
91
```

The value of 89 got printed one only, obviously this is not the best example on where to use the set() method but you get the idea on when you need to use it.

9-A list of dictionaries:

```
mikasa = {"power" : 91, "intellect" : 80,}
commander_erwin = {"power" : 75,  "intellect" : 97}
captain_levi = {"power" : "96", "intellect" : "85"}

characters = [mikasa, commander_erwin, captain_levi]
for character_ability in characters:
    print(character_ability)
        output
{'power': 91, 'intellect': 80}
{'power': 75, 'intellect': 97}
{'power': '96', 'intellect': '85'}
```

10-A list in a dictionary:

```python
scouts = {
        "elit" : [
                    "captain levi",
                    "commander erwin",
                    "section commander hange"
            ],
        "rookies" : [
                    "kone",
                    "sasha",
                    "historia"]
        }
print("The Elits are:")
for elit_scout in scouts["elit"]:
    print("\t" + elit_scout.title())

print("\nThe Rookies are:")
for rookie in scouts["rookies"]:
    print("\t" + rookie.title())
        output
The elits soldiers are:
    Captain Levi
    Commander Erwin
    Section Commander Hange


The rookies are:
    Kone
    Sasha
    Historia
```

note:

you should not nest lists and dictionaries too deeply,
most likely there's a simpler way to solve the problem.

11-A dictionary in a dictionary:

note:

nesting a dictionary in a dictionary can get complicated
pretty quickly

```
scouts = {
        "captain levi": {
                        "power" : "96",
                        "intellect" : "85"
                        },
        "commander erwin": {
                        "power" : 75,
                        "intellect" : 97
                        },
        }
for scout,scout_ability in scouts.items():
    print("\nName: " + scout.title())
    power_ability = scout_ability["power"]
    intellect_ability = scout_ability["intellect"]
    print("Power: " + str(power_ability) \
        + "\nIntellect: " + str(intellect_ability))
     Output

Name: Captain Levi
Power: 96
Intellect: 85

Name: Commander Erwin
Power: 75
Intellect: 97
```

Chapter 7: User input and while loop

note:

> you can use your prompt in a variable and pass that variable to the `input()`.

```
prompt = ("what's your name rookie? ")
name = input(prompt)
print(name)
print("welcome to the scouts " \
    + name + ", you have my utmost respect")
   output
what's your name rookie? Armin #the user wrote Armin
Armin
welcome to the scouts Armin, you have my utmost respect
```

note:

- Use `raw_input()` if you want the user to input a str type.
- Use `input()` if you want the user to input an integer or float type

1-The module operator (%):
It divides a number by another number and returns he reminder.

> Useful to know if a number is even or odd.

2-Introducing the while loops:
The `for` loop takes a collection of items and executes a block of code once for each item in the collection. In contrast, the `while` loop runs as long as, or while a certain condition is `True`.

3-The while loop in action:

```
protagonists_number = 1
while protagonists_number <= 3:
    print(protagonists_number)
    protagonists_number += 1
        output
1
2
3
```

note:

the programs we use everyday most likely contains while loops, for example while we don't quit the program the program keeps running

4-letting the use to choose when to quit:

```
prompt = "say anything cadet and i will repeat it\n"
prompt+= " or type 'quit' to leave\n"
message = input(prompt)
while message != 'quit':
    print(message)
    message = input(prompt)
        output
say anything cadet and i will repeat it
 or type 'quit' to leave
I ate the potato because it was hot and begging to be
eating, sir #input

I ate the potato because it was hot and begging to be
eating, sir #while loop repeating the message

say anything cadet and i will repeat it
 or type 'quit' to leave
```

5-Using a flag:

useful for complicated programs such as games where multiple event end the game.

- For a program that should run as long as many conditions are True, we use a variable called a flag that acts as a signal to the program.

```
prompt = "say anything cadet and i will repeat it\n"
prompt+= " or type 'quit' to leave\n"
message = input(prompt) + "\n"
active = True #this is the flag
if message == 'quit':
    active = False
else:
    print(message)
        output
say anything cadet and i will repeat it
 or type 'quit' to leave
lol
lol
say anything cadet and i will repeat it
 or type 'quit' to leave
lol
lol
say anything cadet and i will repeat it
 or type 'quit' to leave
quit #the program ends
```

6-using break to exit a loop:

```
prompt = "type any character you know in AoT and the pro
grame will repeat it\n"
prompt+= " or type 'quit' to leave\n"
while True:
    character = input(prompt)
    if character == 'quit':
        break
    else:
        print(character.title())
      output
type any character you know in AoT and the programe will
repeat it

 or type 'quit' to leave

erwin

Erwin

type any character you know in AoT and the programe will
repeat it

 or type 'quit' to leave

hange

Hange

type any character you know in AoT and the programe will
repeat it

 or type 'quit' to leave

quit #the program ends
```

a loop that starts with `while True` will run forever
unless it reaches a `break` statement.

The `break` statement directs the flow of your program, so
you can control which lines of code are executed and

which aren't, the program only executes code that you
want it to, when you want it to.

note:

you can use the `break` statement in any of python's
loops, such as the for loop

7-using continue in a loop:

Rather than breaking out of a loop entirely without
executing the rest of its code, you can use `continue`
statement to return to the beginning of the loop based
on the result of a conditional test, for example,
consider a loop that counts from 1 to 10 prints odd
numbers in the range.

```python
current_number_scouts= 0
while current_number_scouts < 10:
    current_number_scouts +=1

    if current_number_scouts %2 ==0:
        continue
    print(current_number_scouts)
        output
1
3
5
7
9
```

8-Using a while loop with lists and dictionaries:

A `for` is effective for looping through a list, but you
shouldn't modify a list inside a `for` loop because python
will have trouble keeping track of the items in the
list. To modify a list as you work through it, use a
`while` loop using `while` loops with lists and dictionaries

allows you to collect, store, and organize lots of input to examine and report later.

9-Removing all instances of specific values from a list:

```
titans = ["armored", "colossal", "armored","female", "beast"]
while 'armored' in titans:
    titans.remove('armored')
print(titans)
        output
['colossal', 'female', 'beast']
```

10-Filling a dictionary with users input:

```
scouts = {}
active_question = True
while active_question == True:
    name = input("\nwhat's your name? ")
    scout = input("what's your favorit character \
in AoT ")
    scouts[name] = scout
    repeat = input("is there someone else who wants to \
participate in the poll? (yes/ no) ")
    if repeat == 'no':
        active_question = False
for name, scout in scouts.items():
    print(name.title() + "'s favorit character is " \
        + scout.title() + ".")
        Output
what's your name? sphinxtwo
what's your favorit character in AoT hange
is there someone else who wants to participate in the
poll? (yes/ no) no
Sphinxone's favorit character is Erwin.
Sphinxtwo's favorit character is Hange.
```

Chapter 8: Functions

1-Arguments and parameters:

```python
def greet_soldier(soldier): #soldier is a parameter
    print("welcome to the scouts " + soldier.title() \
        + "!, you have proven yourself courages, \
 you have my utmost respect!")
greet_soldier("jean") #jean is an argument
        output
welcome to the scouts Jean!, you have proven yourself co
urages, you have my utmost respect!
```

note:

> When you define a function and write something between
> its parenthesis, that is called a parameter, but when
> you call the function the thing inside the parenthesis
> is called an argument.

2-Passing arguments:
Positional arguments:

which need to be in the same order the parameters were
written

```python
def soldier_info(rank, name):
    print("I am " + rank.title() \
        + " " + name.title() + ".")

soldier_info('commander', 'erwin')
        output
I am Commander Erwin.
```

where each argument consists of a variable name and a
value; and lists and dictionaries of values

```python
def soldier_info(rank, name):
    print("I am " + rank.title() \
        + " " + name.title() + ".")

soldier_info(rank='section commander',
             name='hange')
        output
I am Section Commander Hange.
```

3-Default values:

When writing a function, you can define a default value
for each parameter.

note:

> the **default** value should always be written after every
> **non-default** value parameters, this will allow python to
> continue interpreting **positional arguments** correctly

```python
def soldier_rank(name, rank='rookie'):
    print("I am " + rank.title() \
        + " " + name.title() + ".")

soldier_rank(name='marlo')
        output
I am Rookie Marlo.
```

4-Return values:

The value the function returns is a return value.

The `return` statement takes a value from inside a function and sends it back to the line that called the function.

5-Returning a simple value:

```python
def get_formatted_name(first_name, last_name):
    full_name = first_name + ' ' + last_name
    return full_name.title()
scout = get_formatted_name('armin', 'arlert')
print(scout)
        output
Armin Arlert
```

6-Making an argument optional:

To make an argument optional we need to give it an empty value (**default value**) and put it as last parameter of the function.

```python
def get_formatted_name(first_name, last_name,
                       regiment=''):
    if regiment:
        full_name = first_name + ' ' + last_name + ': '
+ regiment
    else:
        full_name = first_name + ' ' + last_name
    return full_name.title()
scout = get_formatted_name('armin', 'arlert')
print(scout)
        output
Armin Arlert
```

33

7-Returning a dictionary:

```python
def soldier_info(first_name, last_name,
                        regiment=''):
    soldier = {"first name" : first_name,
               "last name" : last_name,
               "regiment" : regiment
               }
    return soldier

soldier_information = soldier_info('armin', 'arlert')

print(soldier_information)
        output
{'first name': 'armin', 'last name': 'arlert',
'regiment': ''}
```

8-Passing a list:

You'll often find it useful to pass a function to a
list, whether it's a list of names, numbers, or more
complex objects such as dictionaries, when you pass a
list to a function, the function gets direct access to
the content of the list.

```python
def ask_soldier(names):
    for name in names:
        question = "why did join the cadetts " \
            + name.title() + " ?"
        print(question)
cadettes = ['armin', 'kone', 'sasha']
ask_soldier(cadettes)
        output
why did join the cadetts Armin ?
why did join the cadetts Kone ?
why did join the cadetts Sasha ?
```

9-Preventing a function from modifying a list:

if you want a function to work with a list but not modify it at the same time, you can instead send a copy of that list to the function As follow:

`function_name(list_name[:])`

note:

> Don't send a copy to a function unless you have a specific reason for that to save memory and time especially when working with large lists

10-Passing an arbitrary number of arguments

You have to add an asterisk before the argument as follow: `def ask_soldier(*names):`

this syntax works no matter how many arguments the function receives.

note:

> the arguments are added into a **tuple**

11-Mixing positional arguments and arbitrary:

`def ask_soldier(names, *other_info)`

note:

> positional and keyword arguments always should come first

12-using arbitrary keyword arguments:

note:

> a parameter with two asterisks before it, will cause python to create an empty dictionary as follow:
> `def ask_soldier(names, **other_info):`

```python
def ask_soldier(first, last, **other_info):

    info = {}
    info['first name'] = first.title()
    info['last name'] = last.title()
    for key, value in other_info.items():
        info[key] = value
    return info

soldier = ask_soldier(
    'jean', 'kirstein',
    regiment='scout',
    reason='wanna do something about the titans')

print(soldier)
        output
{'first name': 'Jean', 'last name': 'Kirstein',
'regiment': 'scout',
'reason': 'wanna do something about the titans'}
```

13-Importing an entire module:

Syntax to import a module: `Import module_name`

The file that you want to import and the file importing the module need to be in the same directory.

Syntax to use a function from an entire module that you imported : `module_name.function_name()`

14-Importing specific functions:

Syntax: `from module_name import function_name`

if you want to `import` more than 1 function just separate

the function names with a comma:

`from module_name import function_name_1, function_name_2`

note:

> with this syntax you just call the function by its name

15-using as to give a function an alias:

note:

> this technic will be useful when you want to import a
> function that has the same name of a variable or
> anything else to avoid confusing and if the functions
> name is too long

syntax: `from module_name import function_name as fn`

note:

> use this technic when ever you call a module, that helps
> readability and clearly a function name is more helpful
> to read than a module name

16-importing all functions in a module:

`from module_name import *`

The asterisk in the import statement tells Python to
copy every function from the module pizza into this
program file. Because every function is imported, you
can call each function by name without using the dot
notation.

note:

> its best not to use this technic when working with
> larger modules that you didn't write: if the module has
> a function name that matches an existing name in your
> project that name will be overwritten.

1. Descriptive names, lowercase, underscores.
2. A comment that explains concisely what the function does, the comment should appear after the definition of the function using docstrings.
3. If you specify default value/keyword arguments no space should be used on either side of the equal sign.
4. Separate functions with 2 blank lines
5. All imports should be at the top of the program, the one exception is to use comments before them.

Chapter 9: Classes:

Creating and using a class:

You can model almost anything using classes.

Lets make a scout class:

List what we know about him

1- name – rank → info
2- agile – brave → behavior

these info and behavior will go in our `scout()` class.

This class will tell python how to make an object representing a scout member. After our class is written we'll use it to make individual instances, each of which represents one specific scout.

note:

- functions inside a class are called methides.
- variables inside a class are called attributes.

```python
class Scout():
    """A simple attempt to model a scout."""

    def __init__(self, name, rank):
        """Initialize name and rank attributes."""
        self.name = name
        self.rank = rank


    def agile(self):
        """Simulate a scout engaging odm gear."""
        print(self.name.title() \
            + " is now engaging odm gear.")


    def brave(self):
        """Simulate a scout attacking a titan."""
        print(self.name.title() \
            + " attacks the titan!")
```

We defined a class Scout(), class names should always be capitalized, __init__ method is a special method that python runs automatically whenever we create a new instance based on the class Scout().

We define the __init__ method to a 3 parameters self, name rank, the self parameter is required and it should come first before the other parameter, it must be included because when python calls the __init__ method later (to create an instance of Scout()), the method calls will automatically pass the self argument. Every method call associated with a class automatically passes self, which is a reference to the instance itself, it gives the individual instant access to the attribute and method in the class

The variable have the prefix *self*, which means they're available to every method in the class, and we'll also be able to access these variables through, any instance created from the class.

The Scout() class have 2 more methods agile() and brave(), because these methods don't need any additional information like name, rank, we just define them to have one parameter *self* to be accessible for instances.

1-Making instances from a class:

```python
class Scout():
    """A simple attempt to model a scout."""

    def __init__(self, name, rank):
        """Initialize name and rank attributes."""
        self.name = name
        self.rank = rank


    def agile(self):
        """Simulate a scout engaging odm gear."""
        print(self.name.title() \
            + " is now engaging odm gear.")


    def brave(self):
        """Simulate a scout attacking a titan."""
        print(self.name.title() \
            + " attacks the titan!")

scout = Scout('levi', 'captain')
print("this scout name is: " + scout.name.title() + ".")
print("his rank is: " + scout.rank.title() + ".")
      output
this scout name is: Levi.
his rank is: Captain.
```

In the line 5 from the bottom of the code We told python to create a scout whose name is Levi and ranked as Captain, when python reads this, it calls the method `__init__` in the Scout() class with the arguments 'levi', 'captain', the `__init__` method creates an instance representing this particular scout and sets the name and rank attributes we provided.

2-Accessing attributes:

We access the attributes by using the dot notation as follow:

```
print(scout.name)
      output
levi
```

3-Calling methods:

after we create an instance from the Scout() class we can use dot notation to call any method inside the class.

```
scout = Scout('levi', 'captain')
scout.agile()
scout.brave()
      output
Levi is now engaging odm gear.
Levi attacks the titan!
```

4-Creating multiple instances:

Even if we use the same name and rank for the second scout, python would still create a separate instance from the Scout() class.

You can make as many instances from one class as long as you give each instance a unique variable name or it occupies a unique spot in a list or dictionary

5-Setting a default value for an attribute:

Every attribute in a class needs an initial value. Even if that value is 0 or an empty string in some cases, such when setting a default value, it makes sense to specify you do this to an attribute, you don't have to include a parameter that attribute.

```python
class Soldier():
    """A simple attempt to model a soldier."""

    def __init__(self, name, rank):
        """Initialize name and rank attributes."""
        self.name = name
        self.rank = rank
        self.regiment = 'scouts'

    def get_regiment(self):
        '''get the rank of a soldier'''
        print("this soldier is from the " \
            + self.regiment.title() + " regiment")


soldier = Soldier('levi', 'captain')
soldier.get_regiment()
        output
this soldier is from the Scouts regiment
```

6-Modifying attributes and values:

you can do it in 3 ways:

1- modifying an attribute's value directly:

```
soldier.regiment='garrison'
soldier.get_regiment()
      output
this soldier is from the Garrison regiment
```

2- modifying an attribute's value through a method:

```
def change_regiment(self , new_regiment):
    """change the default regiment"""
    self.regiment = new_regiment
      output
this soldier is from the Military Police regiment
```

3- incrementing an attribute's value through a method:

```
class Soldier():
    """A simple attempt to model a soldier."""

    def __init__(self, name, rank):
        """Initialize name and rank attributes."""
        self.name = name
        self.rank = rank
        self.regiment = 'scouts'
        self.age = 0

    def soldier_age(self, new_age):
        self.age += new_age
        print(self.age)

soldier = Soldier('levi', 'captain')
soldier.soldier_age(30)
      output
30
```

7-Inheritance:

You don't have always start from scratch when writing a class, if the class you're writing is a specialized version of another class you wrote already, you can use inheritance.

The new class inherited of the previous class is called **child class**, it takes all attributes and method from the previous class (**the parent class**) and have the ability to add more attributes and methods.

```python
class Scout(Soldier):
    """Represent aspects of a car, specific to electric vehicles."""

    def __init__(self, name, rank):
        """Initialize attributes of the parent class."""
        super().__init__(name, rank)

levi = Scout('levi', 'captain')
levi.soldier_age(30)
        output
this soldier age is: 30
```

8-Defining methods and attributes for the child class:

when you define a new attribute in the child class, it won't be associated with any instances of the parent class.

9-Overriding methods from the parent class:

To override a method from the parent class you just have to create a method in the child class with same name of the method you want to override.

10-Instances as attributes:

When modeling something from the real world in code, the class will get lengthy, so its best to split the class to more specified classes.

11-Importing multiple classes from a module:

```
from module import Class1, Class2
```

note:

```
self.admin = Privleges()
```

when an attribute from a class, receives another class, you can use that attribute to access the other class's methods or attributes

12-The python standard library:

The python library is a set of modules included with every python installation.

For example the class OrderedDict from collections.

This class will keep track of the order in which key_value pair are added.

```
from collections import OrderedDict
favorite_characters = OrderedDict()
favorite_characters['erwin'] = 'scout'
favorite_characters['jean'] = 'scout'
favorite_characters['annie'] = 'marley'

for name, regiment in favorite_characters.items():
    print(name.title() + " a favorit : " +
    regiment.title() + ".")
      output
Erwin is a favorit character of mine he's from: Scout.
Jean is a favorit character of mine he's from: Scout.
Annie is a favorit character of mine he's from: Marley.
```

note:

> the module random contains functions that generates random numbers in a variety of ways, it could be useful

Chapter 10: Files and Exceptions:

1-Reading an entire file:

read a file from the same directory:

To begin, we need a file with a few lines of text in it. Let's create a file that has 30 numbers with 10 decimal places per line, and save it in the same directory as the program we're running.

1684231584

4810645120

3647536124

This is the file with the digits, we saved it as digits.txt

```
with open('digits.txt') as file_object:
    content = file_object.read()
    print(content)
        output
1684231584
4810645120
3647536124
```

A directory that contains two directories one for .py and one for .txt:

Save the previous digit.txt in another folder.

```
file_path = r"C:\Users\Erwin\Desktop\scouts\digits.txt"

with open(file_path) as file_object:
    content = file_object.read()
    print(content)
        output
1684231584
4810645120
3647536124
```

Reading line by line:

```
file_path = r"C:\Users\Erwin\Desktop\scouts\digits.txt"

with open(file_path) as file_object:
    for line in file_object:
        print(line)
        output
1684231584

4810645120

3647536124
```

2-Making a list of lines from a file:

```
file_path = r"C:\Users\Erwin\Desktop\scouts\digits.txt"
with open(file_path) as file_object:
    lines = file_object.readlines()

for line in lines:
    print(line.rstrip())
        output
1684231584
4810645120
3647536124
```

3-Working with a file's content:

After you've read a file into your memory, you can do whatever you want with the data.

Lets build a single string containing all the digits

```
file_path = r"C:\Users\Erwin \Desktop\scouts\digits.txt"
with open(file_path) as file_object:
    lines = file_object.readlines()
for line in lines:
    print(line.rstrip())

random_digits = ''
for line in lines:
    random_digits += line.rstrip()
print(random_digits)
print(len(random_digits))
        output
1684231584
4810645120
3647536124
168423158448106451203647536124 #List
30 #Length
```

4-Large files: one million digits:

We keep the same, but we change the text file.

If we want to print the first 5 digits.

```
print(random_digits[:5])
```

5-Writing to an empty file:

you can call `open` with two arguments, file_path +

- `'w'` : to write.
- `'r'` : to read.
- `'a'` : to append.
- `'r+'`: to write and read.

If you omit the second argument python opens the file in read only.

note:

> python can only write strings to a text file, if you want to write numbers you need to convert with `str()`

6-Writing multiple lines:

all you have to do is include the new line character.

7-Exceptions:

Using the try-except block:

```python
first_number = 5
second_number = 0
try:
    answer = int(first_number) / int(second_number)

except ZeroDivisionError:
    print("you can't divide by 0")

else:
    print(answer)
        output
you can't divide by 0
```

if the value of `second_number = 1`:

```python
second_number = 1
        output
5.0
```

FileNotFoundError:

```python
soldier_name = 'marco'
try:
    with open(soldier_name) as file_object:
        content = file_object.read()
except FileNotFoundError:
    message = "sorry, the soldier " \
        + soldier_name.title() + " does not exist."
    print(message)
        output
sorry, the soldier Marco does not exist.
```

8-Failing silently:

To make a program fail silently a write `try` block and in the exception block write `pass`.

note:

> you can use the pass statement as a place holder for anything you want to do later

9-Storing data:

The json module allows you to dump simple python data structures into a file and load that data from that file the next time the program runs.

You can do that with the two json functions.

```
json.dump
json.load
```

Chapter 11: Testing your code:

You need to import the `unittest` module.

```python
import unittest
def soldier_formatted_name(first, last):
    """Make a formatted full name."""
    full_name = first + ' ' + last
    return full_name.title()


class NamesTestCase(unittest.TestCase):
    """Tests for the code."""
    def test_first_last_name(self):
        """Do names like \
            'Jean Kierstein' work?"""
        formatted_name = \
            soldier_formatted_name('Jean', 'Kierstein')
        self.assertEqual(\
            formatted_name, 'Jean Kierstein')

unittest.main()
        output
.
---------------------------------------------------------
--------------
Ran 1 test in 0.000s

OK
```

note:

a passing test prints a dot
A test that results in an error prints an E
A test that results in a failed assertion prints an F

`assert` methods available from the `unittest` module.

method	Use
assertEqual(a, b)	Verifies that a == B
assertNotEqual(a, b)	Verifies that a != b
assertTrue(x)	Verifies that x True
assertFalse(x)	Verifies that x is False
assertin(item, list)	Verifies that item is in list
assertNotIn(item, list)	Verifies that item isn't not in list

The setup() method:

It creates an instance for every 'test_' method in the class, to help you run your tests easier.

```python
class Person:
    def allowed_to_buy_alcohol(self,
      birthday, alcohol_percentage):
        # age 16-18: < 16.5%
        # age 18 and over: > 16.5%
        pass

    def allowed_to_buy_tobacco(self,
      birthday):
        # age 18 and over
        pass
```

we saved this class in a library folder.

```python
import unittest
from library.person import Person


class TestAllowedToBuyAlcohol(unittest.TestCase):
    def setUp(self) -> None:
        self.__person = Person()

    def tearDown(self) -> None:
        del self.__person

    def test_age_are_to_low_to_buy(self):
        self.assertEqual(True,
          self.__person.allowed_to_buy_alcohol('', 4.6))

    def test_age_its_allowed_to_buy(self):
        self.assertEqual(True,
          self.__person.allowed_to_buy_alcohol('', 46.6))


if __name__ == '__main__':
    unittest.main()
        output
```

```
-------------------------------------------------------------
--------------
Ran 2 tests in 0.001s

FAILED (failures=2)
```

We use the `setUp()` method so we can setup something we
need to use later with the cases, and when we are done
we can use the `tearDown()` method to make sure its
cleaned up and we cannot use it anymore.

note:

The `setUp()` method always runs before the test cases and
the `tearDown()` method always runs after the cases

54

Huge Thanks for the Book Cover Designers:

Vecteezy.com

Freepik.com